D1005710

Cats on Quilts

Cats on Quilts

by Sandi Fox

HARRY N. ABRAMS, INC., PUBLISHERS

Project Manager: Ruth A. Peltason
Editor: Ellen Cohen
Design Coordinator: Carol Robson
Designer: Gilda Hannah

Excerpt on page 50 from *To Kill a Mockingbird* by Harper Lee.
Copyright © 1960 by Harper Lee. Copyright renewed © 1988 by
Harper Lee. Reprinted by permission of HarperCollins Publishers, Inc.

Excerpt on page 82 from *Little Women* by Louisa May Alcott.
Reprinted by permission of Little, Brown and Company.

Excerpt on page 106 from *The Tale of Tom Kitten* by Beatrix Potter.
Copyright © Frederick Warne & Co., 1907. Reproduced by kind
permission of Frederick Warne & Co.

Library of Congress Cataloging-in-Publication Data

Fox, Sandi.
    Cats on quilts / by Sandi Fox
      p. cm.
    ISBN 0–8109–5725–6
    1. Quilts—United States—Themes, motives. 2. Cats in art.
3. Cats in literature. I. Title.

NK9112 .F675 2000
746.46–dc21   00–26992

Printed and bound in Hong Kong

 Harry N. Abrams, Inc.
100 Fifth Avenue
New York, N.Y. 10011
www.abramsbooks.com

This book is for my mother, Lucille Ralston, and for my grandmothers, Henrietta Schach and Gertrude Schlack, and for my great-grandmother, Carrie Atherton Wills, who made quilts and loved cats.

Photograph of Carrie Atherton Wills. Wisner, Nebraska; c. 1940. Photographer unknown. 4½ x 6½ in. (11.4 x 16.5 cm). Collection of the author

ACKNOWLEDGMENTS

For over two decades, I have been expressing my gratitude to many of the following colleagues and collectors; every book I have written during those remarkable years has been dependent in large part on their great generosity in helping me secure the perfect images. Once again, I thank them all: Abby Aldrich Rockefeller Folk Art Center/Barbara Luck and Catherine Grosfils, America Hurrah/Kate and Joel Kopp, Darwin Bearley, Banner County Historical Society/Mary Penick, Cheyenne County Historical Association/Ada Ammerman and Robert Buhrdorf, Tom Cuff, Charlotte Ekback, Laura Fisher, Susan Gray, Ann Hoenigswald and Nick Thorner, Robert and Ardis James, Roderick Kiracofe, Rosalind and Ken Landis, Mary Landkamer, Los Angeles County Museum of Art/Steve Oliver, Metropolitan Museum of Art/Deanna Cross and Amelia Peck, Marie Michal and Peter Lubalin, Michigan State University Museum/LaNeysa V. Harris-Featherstone, James and Judith Milne, Museum of American Folk Art/Janey Fire and Gerald Wertkin, North Platte Valley Museum/Lillis Grassmick, Oakland Museum of California/Inez Brooks-Meyer, Susan Parrish, Pilgrim/Roy/Gerald Roy, Plains Historical Museum/B. Stendahl, Putnam County Historical Society and Foundry School Museum/Charlotte Eaton, Shelburne Museum/Celia Oliver and Robyn Woodworth, Smithsonian Institution/Doris Bowman, Sotheby's/Nancy Druckman, Woodard & Greenstein/Blanche Greenstein and Tom Woodard.

This book has been a cross-country collaboration: In Utah, Emily Lowe found a fine family of cunning cats and kittens hiding on the fiction shelves of the Salt Lake City Public Library: I am very grateful indeed for her research assistance and for our friendship; in New York, my agent, Rita Rosenkranz, and I had talked about this book for years, and Ruth Peltason, my editor at Abrams, looked at the project with clever cat's eyes when it finally reached her desk; and in Los Angeles, as he has done for four decades, my husband, John, made sure that no black cats crossed my path.

The Stylized Cat
A History in Quilts

In ancient Egypt the cat was a deity. Her domestication probably occurred about 1500 B.C., at the beginning of the eighteenth dynasty; it is recorded there on tomb paintings, where she hunts for birds in fading marshlands and where she sits as a talisman of fertility beneath her owner's chair. By the nineteenth century, the continuing threads of that domestication were being sewn into America's quilts and bedcovers.

When the cat moved to Europe, she took with her an image with which she had been associated in Egypt, the sistrum, a four-stringed instrument; no doubt this led to the medieval portrayal of cats playing fiddles. The four elements of the ancient fertility rites that had been practiced in the Nile Delta at the temple in Bubastis—the cat-goddess (Bastet), the sistrum, the cow goddess (Hathor), and the moon—are in fact brought together in a nursery rhyme of undetermined age and origin:

Hey diddle diddle!
The cat and the fiddle,
The cow jumped over the moon.
The little dog laughed
To see such craft,
And the dish ran away with the spoon.[1]

Fig. 1. Quilt Top (detail). Provenance unknown; c. 1935.
Maker unidentified. Cotton, 69 x 48 in. (175.3 x 121.9 cm).
Private collection

Is the Puss in Boots who plays on this early twentieth-century
quilt block (fig. 1) the progeny of Bastet?

During the Renaissance, the invention of printing and the desire of people to read led to an extraordinary increase in the number and nature of books and pamphlets that were available to ordinary men and women.[2] In addition to popular literature, drama, instructional material, and tales of adventure and discovery (all in which cats occasionally played a peripheral role), there was also a great interest in natural history. The medieval bestiaries that delighted the imaginations of the upper classes were replaced by more conscientious and scientific renderings of animals, and these were available to persons of more modest means. In Germany, Albrecht Dürer had brought woodcut book illustration to its acme. This technique was used to present a classic image of the cat (fig. 2) in a pose of inscrutable demeanor— "Pussy was a goddess in old Egypt and she has never forgotten it."[3] Sitting on her regal haunches, tail curled 'round, she assumes the simple shape and stance of an infinitely complex creature, and centuries later that image was duplicated throughout American folk and decorative arts (fig. 3) and eventually on American quilts.

In the fifth century, when Roman occupation ended in Britain, the cats that had lived in the conquerors' forts

Fig. 2. Illustration from Konrad Gesner, *Curious Woodcuts of Fanciful and Real Beasts: A selection of 190 sixteenth-century woodcuts from Gesner and Topsell's natural histories* (New York: Dover Publications, 1971)

Fig. 3. Chalkware cats. Provenance unknown; nineteenth century. Maker unidentified. Polychrome painted surfaces, height 18 in. (45.7 cm). Photograph courtesy Sotheby's, New York

and in their country villas were abandoned to live feral. The descendants of those wild cats still roamed in the nineteenth century, but they no longer bore the stigma placed on them in the Middle Ages when they were considered to be the demonic "familiars" of witches. Finally, when Queen Victoria brought her own cats into her intimate domestic surroundings, her great popular influence assured that the cat had completed the move from Egyptian palace to English parlor.

Cats were still mousers, but the great granaries they had guarded in Egypt were now the barns and fields of rural America. They were often allowed a place in the warm kitchen, occasionally keeping company with a caged bird. Even the adored creature who had been elevated to the position of parlor pet might occasionally lay a tasty morsel at the foot of her mistress. She remained a cat, yet she became significantly more. The cat was not merely an enigmatic presence at the fireside, but an agent for the development of Victorian sensibilities: "Let the little people have their live pets, by all means, even though they do give some trouble and care. Girls must have something to love, and boys something to busy themselves about." (*Godey's Lady's Book,* 1861) "It is indeed remarkable how much these animals can be taught if taken in kittenhood and treated gently." (*Godey's Lady's Book,* 1895)

In addition to the cat, with its physical presence and its instructive possibilities, children themselves were often considered to be their parents' pets and were often called by names such as "Pet" or "Kitten."

The Victorian home, in which the cat was omnipresent, was the domain of the predominantly middle-class woman who was America's quiltmaker. The cat's image was on her walls (fig. 4) and on her bookshelf; its adored self was in her garden or curled comfortably in her lap; thus it seems only natural that this treasured ele-

Fig. 4. "Cat and Kittens." America; probably 1846–65. Artist unidentified. Watercolor and pencil on wove paper, 10 x 13^{15}/$_{16}$ in. (25.4 x 35.4 cm). Collection Abby Aldrich Rockefeller Folk Art Center, Williamsburg, Virginia

ment of her domestic circle should be a subject for frequent and fanciful depiction on her quilts and bedcovers.

Early American quilts of the late-eighteenth and early-nineteenth centuries were most often a reflection of English taste and preferences: vastly intricate, quilted surfaces on richly glazed cala-manco; rich pieces of imported chintz cut out and elaborately applied to a plain cotton ground, in new and inventive floral arrangements, for example. The cat was not noticeably visible on quilts during these early decades, except perhaps on a bit of print-ed toile. By the middle of the nineteenth century, however, a cre-ative confidence became increasingly apparent in the work of American quiltmakers; stunning geometric masterpieces would come to define, for many, this area of American design. It was then, also, that appliquéd pictorial quilts began to appear in increasing numbers.[4] Detailed figures and vignettes often por-trayed elements of a new and vigorous nation and, as in other aspects of American folk art, the art in which Americans took greatest pleasure was that which portrayed themselves and their surroundings. And whether as a part of the narrative scene, or as a single image on the block of a sentimental friendship album quilt, the cat appeared in significant numbers.

Although the great majority of quilts were pieced, few cat designs were worked using that technique (and those few mostly in the early twentieth century). The curving, sinuous lines of the cat were more easily—and perhaps appropriately—rendered in appliqué:

Cats, no less liquid than their shadows,
Offer no angles to the wind.
They slip, diminished, neat, through loopholes
Less than themselves.[5]

In the closing decades of the nineteenth century, a new genre entered into the vocabulary and efforts of the American quilt-maker: Crazy Quilt! The energetic enthusiasm for Japonisme that swept America following the installation of the Japanese exhibit at the 1876 Centennial Exhibition in Philadelphia; an intense interest in the Aesthetic Art Movement in England; the work of the English art-needlework societies (their work also present in Philadelphia)—all were among those creative influences that altered the more orderly surfaces of America's quilts. Up to the last quarter of the century, those surfaces had been stylized with floral appliqué or wonderfully inventive geometric patterns—squares and rectangles and diamond shapes, sewn with tight little running stitches into the American pieced quilt. Then, in the manner of the Japanese, all symmetry was obscured; the quilt's surface became a fantastic jumble of angles and overlapping seams—those seams covered with elaborate combinations of embroidery stitches—and the face of the patches themselves adorned with an extraordinary range of images. Those images were primarily floral: the tiny sprigs of America's gardens, delicate and diverse; the more flamboyant blooms that Oscar Wilde carried or wore in his lapel as he toured the United States in the early 1880s. Figurative motifs drawn from the Aesthetic Movement were particularly favored: insects, fans, owls, cranes, and Kate Greenaway–style figures, for example. Cats and kittens crept among them all. Some appeared on snippets of manufactured ribbons, often in humorous situations; others were drawn freehand in the simplest of shapes—embroidered echoes of chalkware cats. Still others were worked from stamping patterns and hot iron-on transfers (fig. 5), commercially drawn designs from the large industry that had been created to cater to American needleworkers.

During roughly the same period, in an opposing simplification of the quilt's surface inspired by the Royal School of Needlework, those stamped or transferred patterns on crazy quilts were elsewhere outlined in Turkey Red embroidery floss on a plain, white ground. This was often the case with the belled and beribboned "Our Cat" pattern, turning up like an old friend on a substantial number of such pieces (see p. 87). Another category of commercial offerings was the preprinted "penny squares," usually presented in thematic series such as birds, Bible stories, and Sunbonnet Babies. Some women preferred to mark their own patterns, occasionally using designs from their child's coloring books. Relatively fast and easy to embroider, the scenes and figures could, however, be exceptionally detailed: historical or equestrian figures, for example, which can often be traced to a variety of more sophisticated print sources such as illustrations from *Harper's Magazine*.

In a yet more simple method of securing the cat's image for her quilt or bedcover, the maker could return to the technique in favor at the beginning of the century, that of cut-out chintz appliqué. In the closing decades of the century, a quiltmaker whose tastes or talents may not have extended to the creation of a complex image might have simply cut desired elements from one of the numerous printed cottons that featured cats in sweet situations (see p. 89); these usually pictured cats or kittens in playful poses, often in or out of baskets.

Fig. 5. "Our Cat" advertisement. From *The Delineator*, June 1885. Collection Library of Congress

The quiltmaker's chosen technique was carefully considered; an older woman sometimes chose a style from her youth rather than the one currently in vogue. The design itself was seldom completely original; if she decided against a commercial pattern, she might look for something she could copy or adapt. The cat became one of the period's most popular subjects in all printed media, offering the quiltmaker an almost overwhelming number of options.

Cats figured prominently in illustrations for books and magazines, of course, and on the covers of sheet music such as "The Black Cat Rag," "Pussy Foot Fox Trot," and "Kitten on the Keys." The new chromolithography produced a seemingly endless number of gloriously colorful cats in poses and situations both beautiful and bizarre; they permeated the great outpouring of Victorian paper products that became a nation's keepsakes. And by the late 1800s, cats appeared in great profusion to sell America's products, providing quiltmakers with inspiration for subject matter and direct sources of design (figs. 6 and 7).

For example, in 1872, when Ephram S. Wells got tired of fighting rats in the basement of his New Jersey home, he produced a potion for their prompt elimination; his wife declared it to be "Rough on Rats," and it was so named. The company advertised widely, including on a trade card that illustrated six cats encircling a can of the deadly product with three wire rat traps hanging uselessly overhead; the caption reads "OUR OCCUPATION GONE 'Rough on Rats Did It.'"[6] In 1904, the Ladies Aid Society of North Highlands Methodist Episcopal Church in Phillipstown, New York, prepared a quilt for a fundraising auction; one block features four red appliquéd cats encircling the inscription "Rough on Rats"!

Cats sold all manner of products, either as a logo (Black Cat

Fig. 6. "It's Comfortable" advertisement. From *Frank Leslie's Popular Monthly*, December 1901. Collection of Library of Congress

Fig. 7. Redwork Bedcover (detail). Probably Pennsylvania; marked 1887. Maker unidentified. Cotton, 89¼ x 77 in. (226.7 x 195.6 cm). Collection Los Angeles County Museum of Art, California. Purchased with funds provided by Aldo and Valerie Bussio, AC 1993.22.2

Stove Polish, Kaliko Kat Shoes, and White Cat Union Suits) or included in an advertisement extolling the virtues of such diverse items as Cosmolac Varnish and Dr. Thomas' Electric Oil Liniment. The art directors of the largest and most reputable of advertising companies took advantage of the cat's universal appeal by including it in ever more clever tableaux; a cat with a paw in a goldfish bowl was particularly popular—a design used also on redwork "penny squares." By the 1900s, the Corticelli Cat was surely one of the most familiar to quiltmakers, for, in addition to a massive advertising campaign for all Corticelli products, that cat appeared on the ends of spools of Corticelli silk and cotton thread—an important component of the quiltmaker's creative life's blood.

By 1880, a good cigar was the most popular tobacco product in the United States, and the boxes in which they were packed (for purposes of tax calculation) led to an elaborate form of point-of-sale advertising—the cigar-box label. The exquisite designs were worked by artisans using a stone-based form of lithography and a thirteen-color process. With the boxes open on the tobacconist's shelves, the prospective purchasers were presented with a panorama of illustrations, from vignettes of domestic life to occasionally seminude women or smoking cowboys, and (of course!) those cats. Always beautiful, and frequently whimsical, cats appeared in significant numbers: "Old Tom," "Tabby," "Pussy," "Our Kitties," and "Cats" playing on a tabletop—a popular subject for the woven ribbons stitched onto crazy quilts. Family members eagerly awaited the eventually empty boxes where, in sewing rooms and playrooms, they often became treasured trinket boxes for women and children.

Tobacco manufacturers provided an additional and more obvious incentive for a woman to encourage her husband's tobacco purchases, and indeed, in the case of cigarettes, to urge women themselves to smoke. The narrow silk ribbons that held bundles of cigars were generally considered somewhat impractical for crazy quilts ("Ned is such an absurd brother! This morning he came in with a lot of those nasty little yellow cigar ribbons all in a tangle, and offered them to me for my crazy quilt."[7]), but some ambitious needlewomen saved them by the hundreds or thousands and sewed them into geometric arrangements for bedcovers and pillow shams. More particularly sought were the premiums inserted in packages of cigarettes, silk and satin illustrations (usually with an identifying word or phrase) of flowers and birds, foreign flags and kings and queens, bathing beauties and Indian Chiefs, cows and dogs and cats. The Player Tobacco Company offered instructions for their useful and artistic employment on bedcovers and elsewhere:

> "The satin inserts may be stitched (herringbone style) on a piece of silk, satin, or other material. As indicated, some simple embroidery adds greatly to the attractiveness of the finished article (see p. 103). Other things that can be made of the inserts are screens, bedspreads, lamp shades, sewing bags, hat bands, portieres, pin cushions, doilies, table centers, masquerade dresses, belts, bands for the hair, kimonos, pillow tops, ties, piano drapes, tablecloths, doll's dresses, teapot cozies, egg cozies, mantel drapes, com-

forters, handkerchief bags, sideboard covers, dresser covers, covers for chairs, parasols, etc."[8]

These were among the fancywork objects that seemed to consume every creative moment of the Victorian housewife's day, and a cat "silkie" may have appeared on many. Women were directed in the conduct of their daily lives and the decoration of their homes by a significant number of women's books and magazines ("female persuaders"), and particularly following the Centennial Exposition, those instructional elements extolled the virtue of turning bits and pieces and small items that might otherwise be thrown away into highly decorated household objects (usually of dubious taste). These "artistic" contributions to her home might serve a secondary purpose: in 1884, *Dorcas Magazine* identified fancywork as "the best and only rest possible to many a nervous woman. Remember, monsieur, she has not the resource of a cigar."

But in addition to the creation of fancywork, women, "nervous" or not, were expected to elevate their mind and to bring art into their lives. They were encouraged in their endeavors by the large number of critical articles and artists' biographies that appeared in women's magazines and through visits to the museums and galleries that were seen as havens of culture in most major American cities. Thus prepared, the wife and mother—as cultural arbiter for her family—could then bring art into the home. This was increasingly possible because of technological developments in printing: ". . . facsimiles of oil or water-color paintings by the best artists, in most cases equal to the originals," could be purchased from Louis

Prang and Company of Boston in 1883, with prices ranging from ten cents for landscapes to fifteen dollars for a large *Madonna* after Murillo.[9] Cats by the old masters, perhaps, on faux canvas. But the most common and comfortable images on Victorian walls were those published by Currier and Ives. The popularity of cats as an image is confirmed by the thirty-eight large-scale lithographs that the company published between 1847 and 1880 featuring cats, with and without children. In fact, there are few Currier and Ives subjects that did not find expression on America's quilts and bedcovers.

As a personal pet, the cat seems always to have been the predominant choice of writers and poets (Edgar Allan Poe's Catalina or Charles Dickens's Willamina, for example), and a writer often worked with his or her cat in close proximity, sometimes on a writing table or even on a shoulder. A quiltmaker surely worked often, or always, with a cat at her side. To confirm the place of the cat in domestic America, we can look to letters and diaries and journals where the pace and pleasures of the quiltmakers' lives were often recorded. Although stylistically we would not expect to see a cat on any of Elizabeth Drinker's quilts, we know from her Quaker Philadelphian diary that Elizabeth (1735–1807) quilted; (20 November 1785, ". . . spent the afternoon at Betsy Moodes: help'd to Quilt: spent the evening at F. Rawle's."[10] September 1799, "Sally Downing is gone to Tommy Downings next door to a quilting match where I was invited, but did not suit me to go . . ."[11]), and that a cat at least occasionally sat by her side: "A very pretty Female Cat, intruded herself on us this evening we did not make her welcome at first, but she seemed to insist on staying, Sall then gave her milk, and very soon after, she caught a poor little mouse, and is now laying on the corner of my Apron by the fireside as familiarly as if she had liv'd with us seven years. William reading, Sall asleep on couch, Sip in kitchen . . ."[12] (5 November 1794).

The elaborate rituals in which the cat had participated in her position of deity were now of a more simple nature, but rituals nevertheless. When the last quilting stitch had been worked on the surface of a quilt, if the actual quilting had been done at a communal quilting bee, a ceremony, which varied regionally, called "Shaking the Cat," sometimes ensued. "A cat was then placed in the middle of the quilt and that young man or woman over whose head it jumped was thereby elected as the next sacrifice on the altar of matrimony."[13]

And the cat sometimes followed the quilt to an upstairs bedroom to become a part of those simple memories from time to time recalled:

"On that night when I went to bed about twelve o'clock I missed Toss, who is generally by the fire in the room where we sit; when I went upstairs there she was sitting upright in the middle of my bed waiting for me. There was no fire in the room, and she never sleeps on our bed, but that night she missed Flu, and came there to inquire for her and to keep me company. She curled herself up on the counterpane by my side."[14]

Cats and quilts are thus both objects of infinite comfort.

* * * * *

Cunning Cats & Kittens

The designs for these cats on quilts have come from diverse sources, and the quilts themselves were likewise worked by diverse hands: an inmate in an asylum in Catonsville, Maryland, in 1850 seems to have constructed her images from those that floated in her troubled mind[15] (see p. 33); a grandmother working in the 1940s on her ranch home thirty miles from Burwell, Nebraska, drew on the simplest techniques and patterns of the American quiltmaking tradition and on a seemingly bottomless scrap bag (see p. 127). By the middle of the twentieth century, much of the quiltmaker's individual creativity had waned: when the Metropolitan Museum of Art commissioned Marion Cheever Whiteside Newton, the owner of a commercial quiltmaking business in New York, to design a quilt for their collection, she turned for her designs (slightly simplified) to the illustrations prepared by Sir John Tenniel (1820–1914) for Lewis Carroll's *Alice's Adventures in Wonderland*, first published in 1866 (fig. 8 and see p. 123). (This approach to design was not new to American needlewomen: a century and a half earlier, schoolgirl embroideries were often based directly on English prints. Technical excellence was considered to be more important than original design.[16]) That which bound these quiltmakers together was their delight in the possibilities of textiles as a creative medium, as well as their shared preference for the image of the cat as a small, dear subject sure to evoke in themselves and others moments of pleasure and remembrance.

Fig. 8. Illustration by Sir John Tenniel, from Lewis Carroll's *Alice's Adventures in Wonderland* (William Morrow & Co., 1992; first published by Macmillan and Co., 1866)

Fig. 9. Fabric Diary. Provenance unknown; nineteenth century. Kept by Eliza A. Tillinghast. Collection America Hurrah Antiques, New York. Photographs courtesy Roderick E. Kiracofe/The American Quilt

Early in the nineteenth century, many young women were taught to draw and to paint, either in dame's schools and academies or in formal classes. Alone, they often consulted self-instructional books and manuals. The skills thus acquired were frequently translated from works on paper onto surfaces of softer stuff. Scraps of the fabrics of her dresses, and those of her family and friends, were often the materials with which the quiltmaker worked her quilts. In the nineteenth century, Eliza A. Tillinghast cut and applied to the

pages of a scrapbook just such fabric. She noted the dates of the clothing ("dress of 1832," "sunbonnet 1835") and sometimes the occasion on which it had been worn: "Eliza Garfield was married to Gideon Tillinghast on Jan. 27, 1847," "Eliza's wedding dress," "wedding coat," "Gideon wedding vest." The cunning cats and kittens she included on her remarkable fabric diary (fig. 9) suggest, perhaps, their special place in her daily life and in her heart. Perhaps they also found enduring homes on her quilts.

ENDNOTES

1. Roger Tabor, *Cats: The Rise of the Cat* (London: BBC Books, 1991), pp. 31–32.

2. See Mary Robertson, *Worlds of Profit and Delight: Popular Reading in Renaissance England* (San Marino, California: The Huntington Library, 1999).

3. Oswald Barron, quoted in Christabel Aberconway, *A Dictionary of Cat Lovers* (London: Michael Joseph, 1950), p. 42.

4. See Sandi Fox, *Wrapped in Glory: Figurative Quilts and Bedcovers 1700–1900* (New York: Los Angeles County Museum of Art and Thames and Hudson, 1990).

5. A. S. J. Tessimond, quoted in Maria Polushkin Robbins, *Puss in Books* (Hopewell, New Jersey: The Ecco Press, 1998), p. 150.

6. See Alice L. Muncaster and Ellen Yanow, *The Cat Made Me Buy It! A Collection of Cats Who Sold Yesterday's Products* (New York: Crown Publisher, Inc., 1984), p. 28.

7. Dulcie Weir, "The Career of a Crazy Quilt," *Godey's Lady's Book and Magazine*. Vol. 6, No. 649, July 1884, p. 78.

8. Cited in Philip Collins, *Smokerama: Classic Tobacco Accoutrements* (San Francisco: Chronicle Books, 1992), p. 56.

9. Harvey Green, *The Light of the Home: An Intimate View of the Lives of Women in Victorian America* (New York: Pantheon Books, 1983), p. 107.

10. Elaine Forman Crane, ed., *The Diary of Elizabeth Drinker* (Boston: Northeastern University Press, 1994), p. 5.

11. Ibid., p. 214.

12. Ibid., pp. 138–39.

13. William Rush Dunton, Jr., *Old Quilts* (Catonsville, Maryland: privately published, 1946), p. 18.

14. Matthew Arnold, quoted in Aberconway, *A Dictionary*, p. 23.

15. Fox, *Wrapped in Glory*, pp. 42–45.

16. Ibid., pp. 76–79.

Cats on Quilts

For I will consider my cat Joeffry . . . .

For in his morning orisons he loves the sun and
the sun loves him.

For he is of the Tribe of Tiger.

For the Cherub Cat is a term of the Angel Tiger.

For he has the subtlety and hissing of a serpent,
which in goodness he suppresses.

For he will not do destruction, if he is well-fed,
neither will he spit without provocation.

For he purrs in thankfulness, when God tells him
he's a good Cat.

For he is an instrument for the children to learn
benevolence upon.

For every house is incomplete without him and a
blessing is lacking in the spirit.

—Christopher Smart (1722–1771),
from "Jubilate Agno"

Quilt (detail). Catonsville, Maryland; c. 1850. Made by a patient at the Spring Grove State Hospital. Cotton, 89 x 79 in. (226 x 200.7 cm). Photograph America Hurrah Archive, New York

Wherever a cat sits, there shall happiness be found.

—Stanley Spencer, (1891–1959)

Quilt Top (detail). Possibly Erie, Pennsylvania; c. 1850.
Block signed Sadia Morehouse. Cotton, 70 x 70 in. (177.8
x 177.8 cm). Collection Susan Parrish Antiques, New York

Of a noble race she came,
And Grimalkin was her name.
Young and old full many a mouse
Felt the prowess of her house;
Weak and strong full many a rat
Cowered beneath her crushing pat;
And the birds around the place
Shrank from her too-close embrace.
But one night, reft of her strength,
She lay down and died at length:
Lay a kitten by her side
In whose life the mother died.
Spare her life and lineage,
Guard her kitten's tender age,
And that kitten's name as wide
Shall be known as hers that died.
And whoever passes by
The poor grave where Puss doth lie,
Softly, softly let him tread
Nor disturb her narrow bed.

—Christina Rossetti (1830–1894),
from "On the Death of a Cat"

Quilt (detail). New York State; c. 1850. Maker unidentified.
Cotton, 88 x 84 in. (223.5 x 213.4 cm). Photograph
America Hurrah Archive, New York

Wild beasts he created later,
Lions with their paws so furious;
In the image of the lion
Made he kittens small and curious.

—Heinrich Heine (1797–1856);
translated by Edward Alfred Bowning,
from *Songs of Creation*

Quilt (detail). Possibly Pennsylvania; c. 1850. Possibly
made by E. Klute. Cotton, 82 x 66 in. (208.3 x 167.6 cm).
Collection Shelburne Museum, Shelburne, Vermont

I saw the most beautiful cat today. It was sitting by the side of the road, its two front feet neatly and graciously together. Then it gravely swished around its tail to completely encircle itself. It was so *fit* and beautifully neat, that gesture, and so self-satisfied—so complacent.

—Anne Morrow Lindbergh (b. 1907)

Bedcover (detail). Doylestown, Pennsylvania; marked 1853. Made by Sarah Ann Garges. Cotton, silk, and wool, 96 x 98 in. (243.8 x 248.9 cm). Collection Museum of American Folk Art, New York. Gift of Warner Communications Inc., 1988.21.01

Housemate, I can think you still
Bounding to the window-sill,
Over which I vaguely see
Your small mound beneath the tree,
Showing in the autumn shade
That you moulder where you played.

—Thomas Hardy (1840–1928),
from "Last Words to a Dumb Friend"

Quilt (detail). Brooklyn, New York; marked 1861 or 1867. Made by friends of Susan Rogers. Cotton, 83⅜ x 85⅛ in. (211.8 x 216.2 cm). Collection Smithsonian Institution, Washington, D.C.

Dear creature by the fire a-purr,
Strange idol, eminently bland,
Miraculous puss! As o'er your fur
I trail a negligible hand.
And gaze into your gazing eyes,
And wonder in a demi-dream
What mystery it is that lies
Behind those slits that glare and gleam.

—Lytton Strachey (1880–1932),
from "The Cat"

Quilt (detail). Brooklyn, New York; marked November 18, 1867.
Made by Lucinda Houstain. Cotton, wool, and silk, 100 x 88 in.
(254 x 223.5 cm). The Robert and Ardis James Collection.
Photograph America Hurrah Archive, New York

Stately, kindly, lordly friend
    Condescend
Here to sit by me, and turn
Glorious eyes that smile and burn,
Golden eyes, love's lustrous meed,
On the golden page I read.

—Algernon Charles Swinburne
(1837–1909), from "To a Cat"

Quilt (detail). Brooklyn, New York; marked November 18, 1867.
Made by Lucinda Houstain. Cotton, wool, and silk, 100 x 88 in.
(254 x 223.5 cm). The Robert and Ardis James Collection.
Photograph America Hurrah Archive, New York

Tom Quartz is certainly the cunningest kitten I have ever seen. He is always playing pranks on Jack, and I get very nervous lest Jack should grow too irritated. The other evening they were both in the library—Jack sleeping before the fire—Tom Quartz scampering about, an exceedingly playful little creature—which is about what he is. He would race across the floor, then jump upon the curtain or play with the tassel. Suddenly he spied Jack and galloped up to him. Jack, looking exceedingly sullen and shame-faced, jumped out of the way and got upon the sofa where Tom Quartz instantly jumped upon him again. Jack suddenly shifted to the other sofa, where Tom Quartz again went after him. Then Jack started for the door, while Tom made a rapid turn under the sofa and around the table, and just as Jack reached the door leaped on his hind-quarters. Jack bounded forward and away and the two went tandem out of the room—Jack not co-operating at all; and about five minutes afterwards Tom Quartz stalked solemnly back.

—President Theodore Roosevelt (1859–1919)
[Personal letter, written in the White House,
to his son Kermit, January 6, 1903]

Bedcover (detail). Possibly North Adams, Massachusetts; c. 1877. Probably
made by members of the Burdick-Childs family. Cotton, 79 x 79 in.
(200.7 x 200.7 cm). Collection Shelburne Museum, Shelburne, Vermont

Miss Caroline began the day by reading us a story about cats. The cats had long conversations with one another, they wore cunning little clothes and lived in a warm house beneath a kitchen stove. By the time Mrs. Cat called the drugstore for an order of chocolate malted mice the class was wriggling like a bucketful of catawba worms. Miss Caroline seemed unaware that the ragged, denim-shirted and flour-sack-skirted first grade, most of whom had chopped cotton and fed hogs from the time they were able to walk, were immune to imaginative literature. Miss Caroline came to the end of the story and said "Oh, my, wasn't that nice?"

—Harper Lee (b. 1926),
from *To Kill a Mockingbird*

Quilt (detail). Probably New York; marked 1879. Maker
unidentified. Cotton, 80 x 80 in. (203.2 x 203.2 cm).
Photograph courtesy Sotheby's, New York

The cat keeps his side of the bargain. . . . He will kill mice, and he will be kind to babies when he is in the house, just so long as they do not pull his tail too hard. But when he has done that, and between times, and when the moon gets up and night comes, he is the Cat that walks by himself, and all places are alike to him. Then he goes out to the Wet Wild Woods or up on the Wet Wild Trees or on the Wet Wild Roofs, waving his wild tail and walking by his wild lone.

—Rudyard Kipling (1865–1936),
from *The Cat Who Walked Alone*

Quilt (detail). Probably New York; marked 1879. Maker
unidentified. Cotton, 80 x 80 in. (203.2 x 203.2 cm).
Photograph courtesy Sotheby's, New York

But with you, man, a cat converses; she coos to you, looks into your eyes, and says: Open, man, this door for me; give me, you much-eating one, from what you are partaking of; stroke me; say something, let me come on to my chair. Towards you she is no wild, solitary shadow; for you she is simply a domestic puss, because she has faith in you. A wild animal is an animal which has no faith. Domestication is simply a state of confidence.

—Karel Capek (1890–1938),
from *I Had a Dog and a Cat*

Child's Quilt (detail). Hillsdale, Columbia County, New York; made for Ida Euretta Cole, born October 29, 1880. Maker unidentified. Cotton, 62 x 52¼ in. (157.5 x 132.7 cm). Collection Marie Michal and Peter Lubalin

I sometimes think the Pussy-Willows grey
Are Angel Kittens who have lost their way,
And every Bulrush on the river bank
A Cat-Tail from some lovely Cat astray.

Sometimes I think perchance that Allah may,
When he created Cats, have thrown away
The Tails He marred in making, and they grew
To Cat-Tails and to Pussy-Willows grey.

—Oliver Herford (1863–1935),
from *The Rubaiyat of a Persian Kitten*

Bedcover (detail). Provenance unknown; c. 1880. Maker
unidentified. Cotton, 82½ x 63 in. (209.6 x 160 cm).
Photograph America Hurrah Archive, New York

She whurleth with her voice, having as many tunes as turnes, for she hath one voice to beg and complain, another to testifie her delight and pleasure, another among her own kind . . . in so much as some have thought that [cats] have a peculiar intelligible language among themselves.

—Edward Topsell (d. 1638?)

Crazy Quilt (detail). Probably Hamilton, Madison County,
New York; c. 1885. Made by Mary Ann Jane (Mrs. Charles H.)
Simmons. Silk and velvet, 70½ x 66½ in. (179.1 x 168.9
cm). Collection North Platte Valley Museum, Gering, Nebraska

I have a Gumbie Cat in mind, her name is
   Jennyanydots;
Her coat is of the tabby kind, with tiger stripes and
   leopard spots.
All days she sits upon the stair or on the steps or on the
   mat:
She sits and sits and sits and sits—and that's what
   makes a Gumbie Cat!

But when the day's hustle and bustle is done,
Then the Gumbie Cat's work is but hardly begun.
And when all the family's in bed and asleep,
She slips down the stairs to the basement to creep.
She is deeply concerned with the ways of the mice—
Their behaviour's not good and their manners not nice;
So when she has got them lined up on the matting,
She teaches them music, crocheting and tatting.

—T. S. Eliot (1888–1965),
from "The Old Gumbie Cat"

Crazy Quilt (detail). Brooklyn Heights, New York;
1886. Made by Florence Elizabeth Marvin. Silk,
velvet, and plush, 80 x 76 in. (203.2 x 193 cm).
Photograph America Hurrah Archive, New York

Mrs. Pipchin had an old black cat, who generally lay coiled upon the centre foot of the fender, purring egotistically, and winking at the fire until the contracted pupils of his eyes were like two notes of admiration. The good old lady might have been—not to record it disrespectfully—a witch, and Paul and the cat her two familiars, as they all sat by the fire together. It would have been quite in keeping with the appearance of the party if they had all sprung up the chimney in a high wind one night, and never been heard of any more.

—Charles Dickens (1812–1870),
from *Dombey and Son*

Crazy Quilt (detail). Probably Fremont, Nebraska; marked 1886. Attributed to Mrs. M. Scott. Silk and velvet, 77½ x 67 in. (196.9 x 170.2 cm). Collection Banner County Historical Society, Harrisburg, Nebraska

I and Pangur Ban, my cat,
'Tis a like task we are at;
Hunting mice is his delight,
Hunting words I sit all night.

Better far than praise of men
'Tis to sit with book and pen;
Pangur bears me no ill will,
He too plies his simple skill.

—Irish monk (8th century),
from "Pangur Ban"

Crazy Quilt (detail). Probably Fremont, Nebraska;
marked 1886. Attributed to Mrs. M. Scott. Silk and
velvet, 77½ x 67 in. (196.9 x 170.2 cm). Collection
Banner County Historical Society, Harrisburg, Nebraska

Last Mayday my cat brought
Into the world six most charming kittens,
Maykittens, all white, with little black tails,
Indeed, it was a lovely childbed!

—Theodor Woldsen Storm (1817–1880),
from "About Cats"

Redwork Bedcover (detail). Probably Pennsylvania; marked 1887.
Maker unidentified. Cotton, 89¼ x 77 in. (226.7 x 195.6 cm).
Collection Los Angeles County Museum of Art, California. Gift of
Aldo and Valerie Bussio, AC 1993.22.2

Through the long orchards of a childhood dream,
Under the blossom-loaded branches of the cherry,
The hunting cat moves with a rippling gleam,
Parting the grass with muscled shoulder, rippled and furry.
Green core to golden eye, love shadowy and late
Under the hot frost of that glancing look—
This is the cat that will crouch, and spring, and sate
The tendoned beast in him, and then at my gate
Will yowl with murmured penitence. I at my book
Will hear, and let him in. Then late, curling
At window ledge, the wise smile cupping the jowl,
He will murmur his sly love, letting hate
Sink down with embered glow through memory's grate,
Knowing the moon will return with freedom, with howl
Of fighters over the wild grass, and soft sound purling
Under the shadowy vines where the lovers wait.

Through all the winding years of childhood moves
This tawny cat I loved, and watched, and fed,
And heard above the sound of sleet and snow,
Prowling the world, while I lay warm in bed.

—George Abbe (1911–1989),
from "Remembered Cat"

Crazy Quilt (detail). Provenance unknown; c. 1890. Maker
unidentified. Silk and velvet, 80 x 68 in. (203.2 x 172.7 cm).
Photograph America Hurrah Archive, New York

Within that porch, across the way,
I see two naked eyes this night;
Two eyes that neither shut nor blink,
Searching my face with a green light.

But cats to me are strange, so strange
I cannot sleep if one is near;
And though I'm sure I see those eyes,
I'm not so sure a body's there!

—William Henry Davies (1871–1940),
from "The Cat"

Quilt (detail). Kentucky; c. 1890. Maker unidentified.
Wool, 93 x 82 in. (236.2 x 208.3 cm). Photograph courtesy
Woodard & Greenstein American Antiques, New York

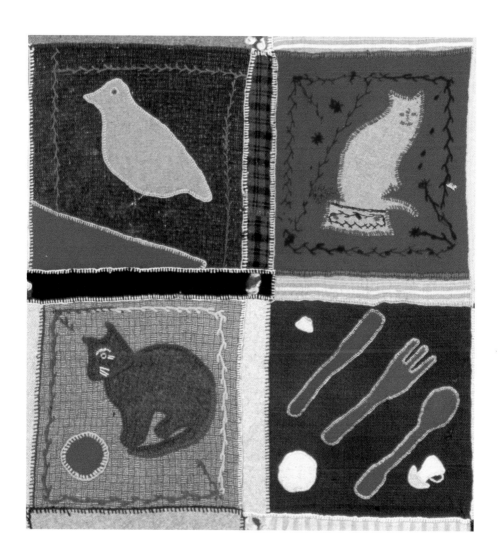

How she beggeth, playeth, leapeth, looketh, catcheth, tosseth with her foot, riseth up to strings held over her head, sometimes creeping, sometimes lying on the back, playing with one foot . . .

—Edward Topsell (d. 1638?)

Crazy Quilt (detail). Provenance unknown; c. 1890.
Marked MV. Silk, velvet, and satin, 50 x 51¼ in. (127
x 130.2 cm). Collection Museum of American Folk Art,
New York. Gift of Margaret Cavigga, 1985.23.08

Sophia says that just before I came home, Min caught a mouse, and was playing with it in the yard. It had got away from her once or twice and she had caught it again, and now it was stealing off again, as she was complacently watching it with her paws tucked under her, when her friend, Riorden's stout cock, stepped up inquisitively, looked down at it with one eye, turning its head, then picked it up by the tail, gave it two or three whacks on the ground, and giving it a dexterous toss in the air, caught it in its open mouth, and it went, head foremost and alive, down its capacious throat in the twinkling of an eye, never to be seen again in this world; Min all the while, with paws comfortably tucked under her, looking on unconcerned. What matters it one mouse, more or less, to her?

—Henry David Thoreau (1817–1862),
from *Autumn*

a bone of contention well removed

Crazy Quilt (detail). Ohio; c. 1890. Maker unidentified. Silk and velvet, 63½ x 56 in. (161.3 x 142.2 cm). Collection Los Angeles County Museum of Art, California. Gift of Mrs. S. B. Milligan and Margaret Milligan. M.79.239.1

She sights a Bird—she chuckles—
She flattens—then she crawls—
She runs without the look of feet—
Her eyes increase to Balls—

Her jaws stir—twitching—hungry—
Her Teeth can hardly stand—
She leaps, but Robin leaped the first—
Ah, Pussy, of the Sand,

The Hopes so juicy ripening—
You almost bathed your Tongue—
When Bliss disclosed a hundred Toes—
And fled with every one—

—Emily Dickinson (1830–1886),
from *The Complete Poems
of Emily Dickinson*

Quilt (detail). Provenance unknown; c. 1890.
Maker unidentified. Cotton, 86½ x 85¾ in.
(219.7 x 217.8 cm). Collection Pilgrim/Roy

With what silent
stealthiness,
With what light steps
do they creep
towards a bird!

—Pliny the Elder (A.D. 23–79)

Quilt (detail). Oakland, California; c. 1893. Made by the
More family children. Cotton, 66 x 54 in. (167.6 x 137.2).
Collection The Oakland Museum of California

She sat poised, air-light, looking, hearing, feeling, smelling, breathing, with all of her, fur, whiskers, ears—everything, in delicate vibration. If a fish is the movement of water embodied, given shape, then cat is a diagram and pattern of subtle air.

Oh cat; I'd say, or pray: be-ooootiful cat! Delicious cat! Exquisite cat! Satiny cat! Cat like a soft owl, cat with paws like moths, jew-elled cat, miraculous cat! Cat, cat, cat, cat.

—Doris Lessing (b. 1919),
from *Particularly Cats*

Child's Pillow Sham (detail). Provenance unknown; fourth quarter nineteenth century. Maker unidentified. Cotton, 16 x 23 in. (40.6 x 58.4 cm). Collection Shelburne Museum, Shelburne, Vermont

THE PUBLIC BEREAVEMENT

It is our painful duty to record the sudden and mysterious disappearance of our cherished friend, Mrs. Snowball Pat Paw. This lovely and beloved cat was the pet of a large circle of warm and admiring friends; for her beauty attracted all eyes, her graces and virtues endeared her to all hearts, and her loss is deeply felt by the whole community.

When last seen, she was sitting at the gate, watching the butcher's cart; and it is feared that some villain, tempted by her charms, basely stole her. Weeks have passed. but no trace of her has been discovered; and we relinquish all hope, tie a black ribbon to her basket, set aside her dish, and weep for her as one lost to us forever.

—Louisa May Alcott (1832–1888),
from *Little Women*

Handkerchief quilt (detail). Provenance unknown; late nineteenth century. Maker unidentified. Cotton, 50 x 44 in. (127 x 111.8 cm). Collection Rosalind and Ken Landis. Courtesy Laura Fisher/Antique Quilts and Americana, New York

Some little Mice sat in a Barn to Spin;
Pussy came by, and popped her head in;
"Shall I come in, and cut your threads off?"
"Oh, no, kind Sir, you will snap our heads off!"

Handkerchief quilt (detail). Provenance unknown; late nineteenth century. Maker unidentified. Cotton, 50 x 44 in. (127 x 111.8 cm). Collection Rosalind and Ken Landis. Courtesy Laura Fisher/Antique Quilts and Americana, New York

Handkerchief quilt (detail). Provenance unknown; late nineteenth century. Maker unidentified. Cotton, 50 x 44 in. (127 x 111.8 cm). Collection Rosalind and Ken Landis. Courtesy Laura Fisher/Antique Quilts and Americana, New York

God made the cat to give
humankind the pleasure of
caressing the tiger.

—Victor Hugo (1802–1885)

Crazy Quilt (detail). Probably Ohio; late nineteenth century.
Maker unidentified. Silk and velvet, 70 x 68 in. (177.8 x
172.7 cm). Collection Judith and James Milne Inc., New York

In a cat's eyes, all things belong to cats.

—English proverb

Quilt (detail). Possibly Massachusetts; c. 1890. Maker unidentified. Cotton, 76 x 75 in. (193 x 190.5 cm). Collection Darwin D. Bearley Antique Quilts, Akron, Ohio

The cat went here and there
And the moon spun round like a top,
And the nearest kin of the moon,
The creeping cat, looked up.
Black Minnaloushe stared at the moon,
For, wander and wail as he would,
The pure cold light in the sky
Troubled his animal blood.
Minnaloushe runs in the grass
Lifting his delicate feet.
Do you dance, Minnaloushe, do you dance?
When two close kindred meet,
What better than call a dance?
Maybe the moon may learn,
Tired of that courtly fashion,
A new dance turn.

—William Butler Yeats (1865–1939),
from "The Cat and the Moon"

Crazy Quilt (detail). Provenance unknown; c. 1900. Maker
unidentified. Silk and velvet, 74 x 52 in. (188 x 132.1
cm). Photograph America Hurrah Archive, New York

If you say 'Hallelujah' to a cat, it will excite no fixed set of fibres in connection with any other set and the cat will exhibit none of the phenomena of consciousness. But if you say 'Me-e-at,' the cat will be there in a moment, for the due connection between the sets of fibres has been established.

—Samuel Butler (1835–1902),
from *Note-books of Samuel Butler*

Crazy Quilt (detail). Provenance unknown; c. 1900. Maker unidentified. Silk and velvet, 74 x 52 in. (188 x 132.1 cm). Photograph America Hurrah Archive, New York

BELLING THE CAT

Long ago, the mice held a general council to consider what measures they could take to outwit their common enemy, the Cat. Some said this, and some said that; but at last a young mouse got up and said he had a proposal to make, which he thought would meet the case. "You will all agree," said he, "that our chief danger consists in the sly and treacherous manner in which the enemy approaches us. Now, if we could receive some signal of her approach, we could easily escape from her. I venture, therefore, to propose that a small bell be procured, and attached by a ribbon round the neck of the Cat. By this means we should always know when she was about, and could easily retire while she was in the neighbourhood."

This proposal met with general applause, until an old mouse got up and said: "That is all very well, but who is to bell the Cat?" The mice looked at one another and nobody spoke. Then the old mouse said:

"It is easy to propose impossible remedies."

—Aesop, from *The Fables of Aesop*

Quilt (detail). Provenance unknown; late nineteenth
century, Maker unidentified. Wool, size unavailable.
Photograph America Hurrah Archive, New York

And that perverted Soul
beneath the Sky
They call the Dog—Heed not his
angry Cry;
Not all his Threats can make
me budge one bit,
Nor all his Empty Bluster
terrify.

—Oliver Herford (1863–1935),
from *The Rubaiyat of a
Persian Kitten*

Quilt (detail). Fluvanna County, Virginia; c. 1900. Made by
Pocahantas Virginia Gay. Wool, silk, and cotton, 68 x 66½ in.
(172.7 x 168.9 cm). Collection Smithsonian Institution,
Washington D.C. Gift of Mrs. Edward McGarvey

*P*uddy is the oldest of the cats. Mostly she sits by the fireside and dreams her dreams. I imagine that she has come to agree with the philosopher that the eye and the ear and the other senses are full of deceit. More and more her mind dwells on the invisible. There was a time when she had her ambitions, when she aspired to be a drawing-room cat. But her looks were always homely, and she became instead a good mother and a good mouser.

—Sir Oliver Lodge (1851–1940),
from *Children of the Moon*, by Moira Meighn

The hough such things may appear to carry an air of fiction with them, it may be depended on that the pupils of her eyes seem to fill up and grow large upon the full of the moon and to decrease again and diminish in brightness on its waning.

—Plutarch (A.D. 46–120)

Quilt (detail). Phillipstown, New York; 1904. Made by the Ladies Aid Society of North Highlands Methodist and Episcopal Church. Cotton, 82 x 73 in. (208.3 x 185.4 cm). Collection Putnam County Historical Society and Foundry School Museum, Cold Spring, New York. Photograph courtesy New York Quilt Project, Museum of American Folk Art, New York

"Tom, Dick and Harry,
Vowed never to marry
"In The Good Old Summer time"
Km Fenton M. Smith

He lies there, purring and dreaming, shifting his limbs now and then in an ecstasy of cushioned comfort. He seems the incarnation of everything soft and silky and velvety, without a sharp edge in his composition, a dreamer whose philosophy is sleep and let sleep; and then, as evening draws on, he goes out into the garden with a red glint in his eyes and slays a drowsy sparrow.

—Saki (1870–1916)

Cigarette Silks Bedcover (detail). East Gloucester, Massachusetts; 1906–1909. Made by Mrs. Charles Ewell. Silk basted to cotton ground, 79 x 68¾ in. (200.7 x 174.6 cm). Collection Los Angeles County Museum of Art, California. American Quilt Research Center Fund, AC 1992.79.1

TABBY CAT

C

was Papa's gray Cat,
Who caught a squeaky Mouse;
She pulled him by his twirly tail
All about the house.

—Edward Lear (1812–1888),
from "Nonsense Calendar"

Crazy Quilt Top (detail). Nebraska; marked 1904.
Block inscribed J.N.V. Wool and cotton, 84 x 71½
in. (213.4 x 181.6 cm). Collection Cheyenne
County Historical Association, Sidney, Nebraska

Mrs. Tabitha dressed Moppet and Mittens in clean pinafores and tuckers; and then she took all sorts of elegant uncomfortable clothes out of a chest of drawers, in order to dress up her son Thomas.

Tom Kitten was very fat, and he had grown; several buttons burst off. His mother sewed them on again.

—Beatrix Potter (1866–1943),
from *The Complete Adventures
of Tom Kitten and His Friends*

In Hans' old Mill his three black cats
Watch his bins for the thieving rats.
Whisker and claw, they crouch in the night,
Their five eyes smouldering green and bright:
Squeaks from the flour sacks, squeaks from where
The cold wind stirs on the empty stair,
Squeaking and scampering, everywhere.
Then down they pounce, now in, now out,
At whisking tail, and sniffling snout;
While lean old Hans he snores away
Till peep of light at break of day;
Then up he climbs to his creaking mill,
Out come his cats all grey with meal—
Jekkel, and Jessup, and one-eyed Jill.

—Walter de la Mare (1873–1956),
from "Five Eyes," *The Complete
Poems of Walter de la Mare*

Quilt (detail, reverse). Nebraska; c. 1925. Made by Agnes (Mrs. Daniel) Freeman. Cotton, 93½ x 72 in. (237.5 x 182.9 cm). Collection Plains Historical Museum, Kimball, Nebraska

We have a cat, a magnificent animal, of the sex which votes, (but not a pole-cat),—so large and powerful that, if he were in the army, he would be called Long Tom. He is a cat of fine disposition, the most irreproachable morals I ever saw thrown away in a cat, and a splendid hunter. He spends his nights, not in social dissipation, but in gathering in rats, mice, flying-squirrels, and also birds. When he first brought me a bird, I told him that it was wrong, and tried to convince him, while he was eating it, that he was doing wrong; for he is a reasonable cat, and understands pretty much everything except the binomial theorem and the time down the cycloidal arc. But with no effect. The killing of birds went on to my great regret and shame.

—Charles Dudley Warner (1829–1900),
from *My Summer in a Garden*

Quilt (detail). Provenance unknown; c. 1930. Maker unidentified.
Cotton, 102 x 80 in. (259.1 x 203.2 cm). Photograph courtesy
Woodard & Greenstein American Antiques, New York

Child's Quilt. Probably Pennsylvania; c. 1925. Maker unidentified.
Cotton, 33½ x 27½ in. (85.1 x 69.9 cm). Collection Museum of
American Folk Art, New York. Gift of Gloria List, 1979.35.01

Child's Quilt. Provenance unknown; c. 1940. Maker unidentified.
Cotton, 46 x 32 in. (116.8 x 81.3 cm). Collection Susan Gray

A black cat dropped soundlessly from a high wall, like a spoonful of dark treacle, and melted under a gate.

—Elizabeth Lemarchand (b. 1906)

Quilt (detail). Hartford, Connecticut; c. 1930. Made by
Mrs. Cecil White. Cotton, 77 x 66 in. (195.6 x 167.6 cm).
Photograph America Hurrah Archive, New York

Mrs. Bird was a timid, blushing little woman, of about four feet in height, and with mild blue eyes, and a peach-blow complexion, and the gentlest, sweetest voice in the world;—as for courage, a moderate-sized cock-turkey had been known to put her to rout at the very first gobble, and a stout house-dog, of moderate capacity, would bring her into subjection merely by a show of his teeth. Her husband and children were her entire world, and in these she ruled more by entreaty and persuasion than by command or argument. There was only one thing that was capable of arousing her, and that provocation came in on the side of her unusually gentle and sympathetic nature;—anything in the shape of cruelty would throw her into a passion, which was the more alarming and inexplicable in proportion to the general softness of her nature. Generally the most indulgent and easy to be entreated of all mothers, still her boys had a very reverent remembrance of a most vehement chastisement she once bestowed on them, because she found them leagued with several graceless boys of the neighborhood, stoning a defenceless kitten.

"I'll tell you what," Master Bill used to say, "I was scared that time. Mother came at me so that I thought she was crazy, and I was whipped and tumbled off to bed, without any supper, before I could get over wondering what had come about; and, after that, I heard mother crying outside the door, which made me feel worse than all the rest. I'll tell you what," he'd say, "we boys never stoned another kitten!"

—Harriet Beecher Stowe (1811–1896), from *Uncle Tom's Cabin*

Quilt (detail). Detroit, Wayne County, Michigan. 1930–36. Made by
Delphine Paulus Miller. Cotton, 81½ x 67½ in. (207 x 171.5 cm).
Collection Michigan State University Museum, East Lansing, Michigan

A
nd the briske Mouse may feast her
selfe with crums
Till that the green-ey'd Kitling comes.

—Robert Herrick (1591–1674),
from "A Country Life"

Quilt (detail). Detroit, Wayne County, Michigan. 1930–36. Made by Delphine Paulus Miller. Cotton, 81½ x 67½ in. (207 x 171.5 cm). Collection Michigan State University Museum, East Lansing, Michigan

A

s I was going to St. Ives,
I met a man with seven wives,
Each wife had seven sacks,
Each sack had seven cats,
Each cat had seven kits:
Kits, cats, sacks, wives,
How many were going to St. Ives?

—Nursery rhyme

Quilt (detail). Possibly Kentucky; 1941–50. Maker
unidentified. Cotton, 83 x 67 in. (210.8 x 170.2 cm).
Collection Museum of American Folk Art, New York. Gift of
Laura Fisher, Antique Quilts and Americana, 1987.08.01

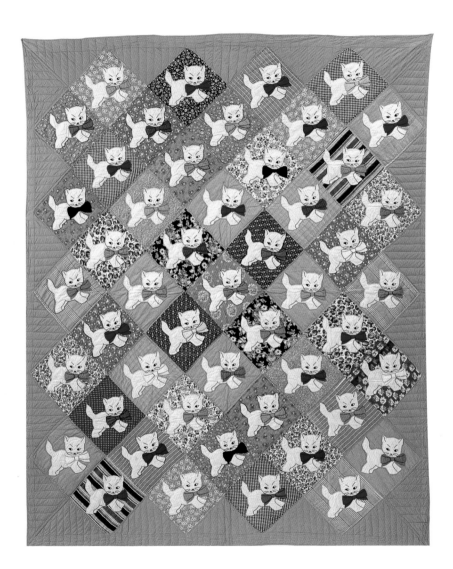

"A

ll right," said the Cat; and this time it vanished quite slowly, beginning with the end of the tail, and ending with the grin, which remained some time after the rest of it had gone.

"Well! I've often seen a cat without a grin," thought Alice; "but a grin without a cat! It's the most curious thing I ever saw in my life!"

—Lewis Carroll (1832–1898),
from *Alice's Adventures in Wonderland*

Child's Quilt (detail). New York, New York; marked 1945.
Designed by, and inscribed, Marion Cheever Whiteside
Newton. Cotton, 65⅝ x 45 in. (166.7 x 114.3 cm).
Collection Metropolitan Museum of Art, New York.
Purchase, Edward C. Moore, Jr. Gift, 1945 45.38

GENTLE MUSINGS ON THE
HOUSEHOLD CAT

"Who let the cat out of the bag?"

"A cat has nine lives."

"That's the cat's pyjamas."

"Not enough room to swing a cat."

"When the cat's away, the mice will play."

Quilt Top (detail). Michigan; c. 1945. Maker unidentified.
Cotton, 60 x 47 in. (152.4 x 119.4 cm). Collection Laura
Fisher/Antique Quilts and Americana, New York

"Ah," says the mother, "we have done some snatchwork on your patchwork. We have thrown it out because it is so very dirty, and we shall buy a basket."

Tabby does not want a basket. She will do some angry scratchwork on it if it comes.

Tabby licks herself and thinks. "I should send this family away and let the milkman stay with me."

She goes to look for her patchwork quilt, to wash herself and stretch and sleep.

She finds it—in the garbage can. She reaches up and touches it. She climbs in under the lid with it and goes to sleep.

Then bang and crash, and black and thick the dark.

The can is in the air and upside down. Tabby falls out, wrapped in her patchwork quilt.

She is in the garbage truck. She cries but no one is there to hear. The engines and the shaking and the quaking drown her calls.

She is going on a journey. She is scared.

—Nicola Bayley,
from *The Patchwork Cat*

Quilt (detail). Vicinity of Burwell, Nebraska; 1942–46.
Made by Jessie Whitney Kelley for her granddaughter,
Mary Landkamer. Cotton, 82 x 74 in. (208.3 x 188 cm).
Collection Mary Landkamer

PHOTOGRAPH CREDITS

Darwin D. Bearley: page 89
Scott Bowron: page 101
John Leslie Fox II: pages 59, 63, 65, 105, 109, 127
Peter Glendinning: pages 117, 119 (© 1987)
Steve Oliver: 1, 7; pages 67, 75, 103
Sharon Risedorph: figure 9; page 99
Sylvia Sarner: pages 35, 83–85, 107, 113, 125
John Bigelow Taylor: page 123